Let's Use

ADVERBS

MARIE ROESSER

Please visit our website, www.enslow.com. For a free color catalog of all our high-quality books, call toll free 1-800-398-2504 or fax 1-877-980-4454.

Library of Congress Cataloging-in-Publication Data
Names: Roesser, Marie, author.
Title: Let's use adverbs / Marie Roesser.
Description: New York : Enslow Publishing, [2023] | Series: Word world | Includes bibliographical references and index.
Identifiers: LCCN 2021042103 (print) | LCCN 2021042104 (ebook) | ISBN 9781978527003 (library binding) | ISBN 9781978526983 (paperback) | ISBN 9781978526990 (set) | ISBN 9781978527010 (ebook)
Subjects: LCSH: English language--Adverb--Juvenile literature.
Classification: LCC PE1325 .R66 2023 (print) | LCC PE1325 (ebook) | DDC 428.2--dc23/eng/20211203
LC record available at https://lccn.loc.gov/2021042103
LC ebook record available at https://lccn.loc.gov/2021042104

Portions of this work were originally authored by Kate Mikoley and published as *Let's Learn Adverbs!*. All new material this edition authored by Marie Roesser.

First Edition

Published in 2023 by
Enslow Publishing
29 E. 21st Street
New York, NY 10010

Copyright © 2023 Enslow Publishing

Designer: Katelyn Reynolds
Interior Layout: Rachel Rising
Editor: Therese Shea

Photo credits: Cover, pp. 1–4, 6, 8, 10, 12, 14, 16, 18, 20, 22–24 iadams/Shutterstock.com; Cover, p. 1 Faberr Ink/Shutterstock.com; Cover, p. 1 Illerlok_xolms/Shutterstock.com; Cover, p. 1 LimitedFont/Shutterstock.com; p. 5 altanaka/Shutterstock.com; pp. 5, 11 Africa Studio/Shutterstock.com; p. 7 David Tadevosian/Shutterstock.com; p. 9 TORWAISTUDIO/Shutterstock.com; p. 13 Vibrant Image Studio/Shutterstock.com; p. 15 Kylbabka/Shutterstock.com; p. 17 Lisa F. Young/Shutterstock.com; p. 19 Halfpoint/Shutterstock.com; p. 21 pixelheadphoto digitalskillet/Shutterstock.com.

All rights reserved. No part of this book may be reproduced in any form without permission in writing from the publisher, except by a reviewer.

Printed in the United States of America

Some of the images in this book illustrate individuals who are models. The depictions do not imply actual situations or events.

CPSIA compliance information: Batch #CSENS23: For further information contact Enslow Publishing, New York, New York, at 1-800-398-2504.

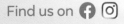

CONTENTS

Useful Adverbs 4
How? 6
When? 8
Where? 10
Aiding Adjectives 12
Adverbs and Adverbs 14
Adverb or Adjective? 16
A Clue 18
Making a Difference 20
Glossary 22
Answer Key 22
For More Information 23
Index 24

Words in the glossary appear in **bold** type the first time they are used in the text.

USEFUL ADVERBS

Adverbs are words that **describe** verbs. Many verbs are actions words, such as *climb* and *jump*. Adverbs tell more about the actions. And that's just one job that adverbs do! Let's learn more. The questions in this book will help. Check your answers on page 22.

HOW?

Adverbs answer some questions. They tell us how or in what way something happened. Read the box below.

> The friends walk together.
>
> The verb, or action, in the sentence above is *walk*. The adverb helps us picture how the friends walk. What is the adverb?

WHEN?

Adverbs can tell us when or how often. They give more **information** about time. Check out this example:

> Sam watched the rain today.
>
> The verb in the sentence above is *watched*. What is the adverb that tells when Sam watched the rain?

WHERE?

Adverbs can tell us where. *Outside, inside, there, here*, and *far* are words that can be adverbs. They help us figure out **location**. Here's one example:

> The kids played outside.
>
> The verb is *played*. What is the adverb that tells us where they played?

AIDING ADJECTIVES

Adverbs tell us more about adjectives too. Adjectives are words that describe **nouns** and **pronouns**. Here's an example of this kind of adverb:

> The very long bus is yellow.
>
> Which adjective does the adverb *very* describe, *long* or *yellow*?

ADVERBS AND ADVERBS

Adverbs also describe other adverbs!

Let's see how:

> The snail moves really slowly.
>
> This sentence has two adverbs: *really* and *slowly*. *Slowly* describes the verb *moves*. Which word does the adverb *really* describe?

ADVERB OR ADJECTIVE?

The same words can be adverbs or adjectives. This box shows how:

> In the sentence below, *high* is an adjective. It describes the noun *score*.
>
> He got a high score.
>
> In the next sentence, *high* is an adverb. It describes the verb *scored*.
>
> He scored high.

A CLUE

Here's a clue to spot some adverbs. Many end with the **suffix** -ly. In fact, these two letters can turn some adjectives into an adverb! For example, the words *quick, loud*, and *sad* are often adjectives. But *quickly, loudly*, and *sadly* are adverbs.

What a quick runner! She runs quickly!

QUICK—ADJECTIVE   QUICKLY—ADVERB

MAKING A DIFFERENCE

Adverbs are important. They aren't just extra words. They can change the meaning of a sentence.

> Tia stopped smiling.
> Tia never stopped smiling.
>
> What a big difference the adverb *never* makes! Adverbs are *really* amazing!

GLOSSARY

describe To tell what something or someone is like.
information Facts about something.
location A place.
noun A person, place, or thing.
pronoun A word used in place of a noun, such as I, you, he, she, it, they, or we.
suffix A letter or group of letters added to the end of a word that changes the word's meaning.

ANSWER KEY

p. 6: together
p. 8: today
p. 10: outside
p. 12: long
p. 14: slowly

FOR MORE INFORMATION

BOOKS
Cleary, Brian P., and Brian Gable. *Dearly, Nearly, Insincerely: What Is an Adverb?* Minneapolis, MN: Lerner Publications, 2022.

Dahl, Michael, and Maira Chiodi. *Adverbs Say "Finally!"* North Mankato, MN: Picture Window Books, 2020.

Heinrichs, Ann. *Adverbs.* Mankato, MN: The Child's World, 2020.

WEBSITES

Parts of Speech
www.dkfindout.com/us/language-arts/parts-speech/
Spot the adverb and learn other parts of speech.

What Are Adverbs?
www.grammar-monster.com/lessons/adverbs.htm
Read much more about helpful adverbs here.

What Is an Adverb?
www.bbc.co.uk/bitesize/topics/zwwp8mn/articles/zgsgxfr
Take the adverb quiz!

Publisher's note to educators and parents: Our editors have carefully reviewed these websites to ensure that they are suitable for students. Many websites change frequently, however, and we cannot guarantee that a site's future contents will continue to meet our high standards of quality and educational value. Be advised that students should be closely supervised whenever they access the internet.

INDEX

adjectives, 12, 16, 18
location, 10
meaning, 20
nouns, 12, 16
pronouns, 12
questions, 6
suffix, 18
time, 8
verbs, 4, 6, 8, 10, 14, 16